Anger in Me

Cheron Van Beek

DEDICATION

Dedicated to Caylee, my rock, my very best friend, my confidante, my everything. Without you, this book would not have come to fruition. Thank you for choosing me to be your mom. Thank you for putting up with me. Thank you for taking this journey with me... I could not have asked for a better person to be with, as my life transforms each day. I wish you all the very best and more for your life! I LOVE YOU!

Mom xox

CONTENTS

INTRODUCTION

"If nothing changes, nothing changes." ~ **Courtney C. Stevens**

Throughout my life, I have faced many trials; some of which have been easier to get through than others. Each trial has left me with my fair share of scars, feelings of guilt, shame, anger and contempt, etc. for the perpetrators. I think it is safe to say that you, too, have had your share of trials in your life, and you are now seeking release from the burdens that have been holding you back. I believe you have been subconsciously led to my book.

I have learned to be grateful for my trials, as I now see how they have played a significant role in returning me to the person I have always been at the very core. I know it sounds crazy to be grateful for trials! No person in their right mind would be grateful for what we perceive to be bad situations in our lives. Trust me when I tell you that being thankful for the bad times is when the most remarkable transformations in you take place.

I have been there. I've often asked the Universe what I ever did to deserve the pain I've experienced. But, once I began to look for the blessing in each situation and found gratitude for it, I slowly began to see changes in me. So many profound changes, that I don't even recognize the person I was before all this began!

I am here to let you know that the situations you have and are facing are situations being used to change your life for the better. They are being used to move you out of your comfort zone and into the greatness you were destined for. If you are anything like me, and don't like change, this may take some time. I'm happy to report that I am learning to embrace change, and a whole lot of other things.

I have to tell you too, that once I stopped fighting the Universe, I began to enjoy the changes I was seeing within me.

During this amazing journey, I have learned some powerful lessons; lessons I will share with you. I ask you to have an open mind, as well as an open heart. Take what speaks to you personally and use that to help you embark on your very own journey of self-love.

1 GRATITUDE CHANGED MY LIFE

My journey to Self-Love has been forty odd years in the making! They say life begins at 40 and I have to agree. My life began to change in the most phenomenal ways in my 43rd year of life on this earth.

Just before I turned forty, I began a romantic relationship with the man I believed to be my lifelong partner. I was finally getting my "happily ever after" it seemed. This happily ever after was going to be short-lived and would forever change my life in ways I had no idea were possible.

You see, before this huge change took place, I thought I was living my very best life, and I was, for who I was back then. The person I was before this great transformation began was not confident, didn't believe in self-love, complained a lot about my life, judged others and myself, thought negatively, allowed fear to hold me back, and certainly never for one minute believed I could ever live the life I AM living now. But the life I was living before this transformation began to take place felt like my best life. I had no idea I was capable of changing, let alone doing the things I AM doing now! But, most importantly, I had no understanding of how much more there really was to me!

Back to my romantic relationship... I had known this man for about seven years prior to our beginning to date. We met through mutual friends, and only saw each other when there was a function being hosted by them. We secretly liked each other, but as life would have it timing wasn't right for us to get together. When he was single, I'd be dating someone else. When I was single, he'd be dating someone else. Eventually, we were both single and began dating in December of 2011.

Due to the fact that we had spent time together on and off for a period of seven years, we decided to try to get pregnant after a few months of dating. I had (still have) a daughter from a previous relationship, who was sixteen at the time. I had been a single mom all these years, and was extremely happy to have found someone who fully accepted my older daughter and took her as his own.

Fortunately for us, we conceived right away. We then decided to move in together, as having two separate places was becoming complicated. We found an apartment and gave notice at our respective places. At this point, I was three months pregnant with our daughter.

Prior to our deciding to move in together, my partner told me he was living in Canada illegally. We made plans to get the move over with, then seek help from an Immigration lawyer on how to proceed going forward. The Universe had different plans for us, because the day before we were set to move in together, my partner was picked up by Immigration Officers, and taken to the Detention Centre.

I remember receiving the call at work, from my partner's friend, telling me that my partner had been picked up. I was devastated! In the blink of an eye my "happily ever after" was pulled from my life. I saw my life being shattered into a billion little pieces. Pieces I was certain I would not be able to put back together.

All at once, many different emotions came over me; disbelief, sadness, fear, shame, anger, disappointment, and worry, to name a few. Then came the questions, "What am I going to do? How am I going to get through this? What did I do to deserve this? How was I going to support two children on my own (a 16-year-old, and an unborn child)? I didn't know what I was going to do. A barrage of thoughts and emotions were going through my mind and my body all at once. I desperately wanted to fall apart, but I was at work, and I didn't want them to know what had just happened. I was too ashamed in the moment, and I needed some time to process what had transpired before I had to face our older daughter.

After my partner's friend called me, I was in total disbelief, so I tried to call my partner on his cell phone. An Immigration Officer answered and told me to bring him some clothes to the detention centre. After the confirmation call, I felt as if I needed some air, so I grabbed my cell phone and went outside. Once outside, I called my sister to tell her what had happened. She was able to help me calm down a bit and helped me get in touch with an Immigration Lawyer. Fortunately, I was able to get an appointment to see the lawyer that afternoon, so I asked to leave work. I can't remember what excuse I used to be able to get the rest of the day off.

I left the office, drove home and packed some clothes for my partner. Then I went to see the lawyer. All this time, I was holding myself together by the grace of God/Universe. At the meeting, the lawyer told me our case should not be too complicated to sort out, and recommended we get married. After meeting with the lawyer, I was finally able to release some of the pent-up emotions by crying all the way home; gut wrenching tears that came from my deepest core of my being. Once again, the grace of God/Universe sustained me and kept me safe on the drive home. I was on one of the busiest freeways (401) at peak hour, driving and crying my heart out!

3

The next task I needed to attend to was to let our sixteen-year-old daughter know what had happened. She had a lot of questions, to which my only answer was, "I don't know." I felt so heartbroken for the both of us. I do not know what her expectations were for this new chapter that had taken such a drastic turn. All I wanted at the time was for the case to be resolved before word got out about what had happened.

This would not be the case. Two weeks later, my partner was deported, and the greatest trial of my life began to take shape. Thankfully, I had been renting the basement apartment from my Canadian family, so our daughter and I were able to remain there. I had to cancel the lease on the apartment we were set to move into, remove some of the stuff we had moved there, as well as remove my partner's belongings from his apartment. Due to the immense shame I felt, I only told a select number of people what had happened, and asked them to keep it a secret.

In July 2012, our older daughter and I met my partner in Cape Town, South Africa, where my partner and I got married. After the wedding, the lawyer submitted our application for Spousal Sponsorship to the Canadian Immigration Office in Vienna. We believed and hoped it would be a couple of months to process the paperwork, and my husband would be able to return to Canada.

By this time, it was two months since my husband was deported, and I was desperate to have him back in Canada before the word got out. I also wasn't looking forward to living my life as a single parent of two children. I just wanted my "happily ever after" back! Was that too much to ask?

As life would have it, our case dragged on for seven years. And, you guessed it, the word got out about what had happened. As every great trial goes, there are those who take great pleasure in humiliating you at every chance they get. My trial was no different. I had my share of humiliators. Each time I attended a social gathering, they brought their humiliation game loud. The person I was back then did not know how to stand up for myself, so I quietly sat there and took the humiliation...for a little while.

After a while, the humiliating social episodes became too much for me to handle on top of all else I was having to deal with, so I withdrew from my social circles. I went into hiding at home, only coming out to go to work or do any shopping I needed to do. At this point, anger at Immigration for the delay in our case began to fester in me. I also became depressed. I hid the depression well, because the person I was before looked down on people who suffered from depression. I was embarrassed to admit that the once "high and mighty Cheron, who thought wallowing in depression was weak," was now facing a deep depression. Another reason I hid the depression, was I knew I had to be strong for our three children, who I was taking care of (yes, a third baby came along. In the summer of 2013, our two daughters and I went to visit my husband in Hungary. It was on this trip that I became pregnant with our third daughter). I also hid the depression, because I was deeply ashamed by it. I was afraid I would be judged and humiliated by others because of it, the same way I had once treated others.

Being constantly humiliated at social gatherings led me stop attending these events. What I didn't know at the time was that these people played a significant role in my life! I know it sounds ludicrous, but it is true. The actions of these people sent me into hiding. It is in the hiding that the dust began to settle and I began to grow, unbeknown to me at the time.

As I mentioned earlier, our case took seven years in total to be resolved. The first four years of the trial felt like the longest and most painful years of my life! In 2016, I came out of hiding. I did not return to the old social circle, but spent lots of time taking my children to the Zoo, Canada's Wonderland, The Exhibition Place, etc. Having fun with my children, as well as experiencing their joy and wonder on our outings, was deeply fulfilling to me.

Things began to change one cloudy day in the summer of 2016. As I made my way home from work, I was stopped at the traffic light, and looked up at the sky. I noticed the sun was shining through the clouds, and thought to myself, "Wow, if the sun in all it's beautiful glory continues to shine behind the clouds, there has to be a "blessing in disguise" in my situation. I don't know what it is, but thank you, God." I honestly did **NOT** feel very grateful at the time, or for a long time after that. From that moment on, though, I began to look at my situation as a "blessing in disguise." Every time, I felt sad or angry, I'd say, "thank you Lord, I know there is a blessing in disguise in my situation. I'm not sure what it is, but thank you."

After five years, our case was rejected, but we were able to put in an appeal. In the meantime, the gratitude for my situation began to change my life. This new way of thinking began to bring new people into my life. People who would love, support, and help me to keep moving forward. The first to arrive back into my life were three of my cousins whom I hadn't been in touch with for a very long time. These three cousins were the first people I openly shared my situation with, outside of my regular support system. They were the first to show me great love and support for my situation. Another cousin had heard through the grapevine what had happened, and always checked up on us from the beginning. At first, I did not see his love and support, because I was blinded by the shame I felt. Eventually, I did see how he was supporting me, and was deeply grateful to him, and my three cousins.

I didn't know it at the time, but the love and support of these four cousins gave me the courage to slowly begin sharing my story with others who began to enter my life. As I was now more positive, instead of being negative, I attracted a Network Marketing opportunity into my life. It was definitely out of character for me to sign up for this opportunity, because I had no idea what being an entrepreneur entailed. As a matter of fact, I thought people who wanted to have their own business were downright crazy! Why would one want to have their own business, when you could go to work, get your paycheck every two weeks, and complain about how much you dislike your boss, your job, and your co-workers, etc?

Although I took the Network Marketing opportunity, I didn't work it, but it did turn out to be a stepping stone for greater things to come, that I wasn't aware of at the time. The Network Marketing opportunity led to the study of personal development. This is when my life really began to change.

My newfound courage allowed me to break free of the stronghold of my regular support system, and begin to explore life on my own with my children. Taking that first small step away from my regular support circle opened me up to more new people who would touch my life differently, and open my heart and mind in ways I never knew were possible. By stepping away from my regular support circle, I was creating space for new people to enter my life. I struggled with this a lot initially! A part of me wanted to be free to explore this new me. At the same time, a part of me was terrified of letting go of them. They had been a significant part of my life and supported me for many years, so I felt guilty. But push forward I did.

Finding gratitude for my trial had set the wheels of transformation in motion, and there was no stopping it. My life had been shattered into a million pieces, because it needed to be rebuilt differently... with self-love, self-care, self-compassion, self-forgiveness, humility, confidence, strength, courage, belief in myself, and so much more!

SOME TOOLS YOU CAN USE:

1. Reach out to someone and ask for help. It is OK to ask for help. It is actually a sign of great **COURAGE**!

2. Find gratitude **for YOUR** situation. I know this sounds completely crazy, but it works. I am living proof of it. However, if you are not yet ready to be grateful for your situation, you can begin by being grateful for the many blessings in your life; your bed, your family, your home, your health, your eye sight, etc. Start with what feels right for YOU!

3. Gratitude is a life changing force/entity.

2 BELIEFS

Although Networking Marketing didn't end up being for me, it was the steppingstone to the study of personal development, which brought people into my life who would allow me to share my story slowly but surely. Sharing my story with strangers who supported me, instead of ridiculing me increased my courage. Personal development brought about a huge transformation that led to internal healing, self-discovery, and reconnecting to the love within me. A love that is in each one of us.

One of my very first lessons in personal development was to address my beliefs. I remember being asked what my beliefs were. I thought this was a crazy question as:

(i) No one had ever asked me what my beliefs were.

(ii) I didn't know anything about how the beliefs I had were limiting my potential in life.

(iii) I had no idea what these so-called beliefs were.

Because my mentor kept harping on about these beliefs, which irritated the hell out of me, I eventually decided to find out what my beliefs were, and where I'd gotten them. I was now eager to discover what was on the other side of these limits I'd lived my life by for so long. I wanted to discover ME ... the real ME! I was curious to see what I was truly capable of achieving, so I set out to find these limiting beliefs and break free of them one by one.

As I began to look into these beliefs, I discovered that they were not my own. They had been handed down to me. Those beliefs are what governed my life and dictated what I would and would not do, how I treated people based on the colour of their skin, how much money I was able to make, and so much more...

The greatest discovery to come out of this was, that I **COULD** change all these beliefs and behaviour patterns. This was a remarkable discovery to me, as I had never thought to question the beliefs I grew up with. I simply inherited them and went along with them!

No sooner did I discover that these beliefs had been handed down to me I then became eager to be free of them. I now wanted more for my life and my children. I looked at those beliefs as a bondage that had been handed down for many generations. Even though I wanted more for my children and I, the driving force behind my desire to be free of this perceived bondage was to free myself from my mom (more on this in the chapter "Anger In Me"). As I grew, I began to understand that if I was going to be more than who I was, then many of the beliefs I had would certainly need to change, as well as be healed in the process.

Some of the major beliefs I had to work on and change were:

- ❖ My beliefs around money.
- ❖ My beliefs about myself and others
- ❖ My segregated mentality (racism within me)
- ❖ My hand-me-down mentality

SOME TOOLS YOU CAN USE:

1. Assess your current beliefs.

2. Ask yourself where you got those beliefs from? Are any of them your own, or have you inherited them?

3. Find out how your beliefs are limiting your life.

4. Do not be afraid to change any beliefs that need to be changed. Do not be afraid to break generational cycles.

3 CHANGE

"Everything is in a constant state of change." ~ **Excerpt from a Healing Energy Piece**

One of the first things I noticed about myself was I was now embracing change whereas before I had always feared it. I feared change so much in the past that I would lose sleep over any upcoming changes I became aware of, especially if they were not ones I wanted for myself. I had always done my best to keep things the same as much as possible. What I didn't recognize was that even though I resisted change, it still took place; having to move house, learning to drive a car, buying a car, and so much more.

This new person I was becoming began to understand how wonderful change really is. I found that there is so much to learn and gain by embracing change. I was learning more about who I really was, and seeing that I was capable of achieving so much more with my life than I ever imagined. I was also becoming open to learning more about others, instead of judging them because they behaved differently than me. I now saw those differences as an opportunity to have my mind and my heart opened to the love of learning. Having my heart opened to learning new things was definitely something new for me, because growing up I always believed I was stupid and that I would not account for much in life. Now, I was uncovering a brilliance within me I didn't know existed underneath all the limiting beliefs doubts and fears. This was definitely something I was open to exploring more!

I began to understand that it is okay to break free of the generational beliefs I had inherited and live my life by new beliefs that aligned with who I AM in each new phase of my life. I began to see how I was changing, and I began to embrace this remarkable journey I was now taking; a profound journey of self-discovery!

Whether we embrace it or not, change is continuously taking place around and within us. I have found that it is a great human habit to remain focused on the past, and how things used to be, which leads to missing out on the profound beauty of the change and the present moment.

The changes that needed to take place have taken place, and the changes that need to take place will do so at the appropriate time. It is our way of thinking we need to focus on changing. Release your strong hold of "the way things used to be" and embrace the way things are now, whilst keeping in mind that change is constant.

SOME TOOLS YOU CAN USE:

1. Don't be afraid to embrace change. Change provides an opportunity to learn something new (which can be a whole lot of fun).

2. By embracing change, you are ultimately taking a chance on YOU!

4 SELF-DISCOVERY

Self-discovery not only changed my beliefs it opened my once closed mind and heart. I was curious to find out who I really was, and what I was capable of achieving. My heart was now open to loving me for who I was.

I began to discover so much about me. I always knew I didn't have much confidence, which led to the discovery of how mean I was to myself in my thoughts. I thought I was stupid, and I constantly body shamed myself. I really wasn't very good to myself. My beliefs in my ability to achieve much in life was lacking greatly.

As I awakened to how mean I was, I was led to another mentor, who turned out to be the BEST mentor ever! She introduced me to the work of the late Louise Hay and the late Dr. Wayne W. Dyer, whose work has been instrumental in my growth. My mentor was exactly who I needed for that period in my life. She was able to see something greater in me that I wasn't able to see in myself. She believed in me far more than I believed in me. She nurtured me lovingly, as well as showed me how to begin loving and believing in myself. Because of her, I was able to keep going on my own, when the journey required alone time.

There were (and still are) a few women who entered my life at the right moment. These women were another great source of love and support to me. Two of them were instrumental in my awakening to the fact that I had a segregated mentality, and that I was racist. I love how instead of judging me when I said derogatory things, they asked me to explain myself. It is in the explanations I gave that I awakened to the racism within me.

My family is from Zimbabwe, and my parents and grandparents lived through segregation. I did too for a while. Even though things began to change, there was still that way of seeing people and making assumptions about every aspect of them based upon their race. I remember many a time my older daughter, who grew up in Canada, would tell me I was racist. I would become highly offended by her remark and yell at her. How things had changed. Here I was changing, seeing life differently, and through some amazing women, I came to the realization that my older daughter had been right all along! I AM deeply grateful to have been awakened to this part of me, because I was able to do the necessary work that was applicable to me and change my behaviour towards other humans. I now see people differently and treat everyone with as much love and respect as I can.

These women were a source of great love to me in the early days. I AM deeply grateful to each one of them. They loved me through the good, the bad and the ugly. Their unconditional love was another powerful source that kept me moving forward. The love they bestowed upon me, was a love that allowed me to figure out the chaos of change that I was going through but didn't initially understand.

I believe it is important to have people in your life who see the greatness in you, way before you discover it for yourself. It is also important to have people who love you unconditionally, instead of judging you. This love gives you the freedom to open yourself up to loving YOU, and accepting YOU for exactly who YOU are.

Because I experienced this profound love, I was able to begin loving myself. I slowly began to love the crazy quirks about me that I was once ashamed of. I was able to see how unique I am, which in turn opened the eyes of my heart to how beautiful and unique others are. It really isn't about trying to be like others... it's about accepting YOU wholeheartedly!

I also began working on releasing the blocks that had held me captive in a life of limitation, I discovered the pure joy of loving me! A love I was initially led to believe was not allowed. My whole life, up to this point, I had believed if you love yourself, you were conceited, vain or haughty...all of which were frowned upon.

The self-love I discovered was not this at all. In fact, it is a love that is pure, wholesome, and deeply fulfilling.

Being able to love myself this way empowered me greatly. It changed me and allowed me to see others through eyes of love, instead of fear of their differences, or judgments of them. This love taught me that we are all different for a reason. Each and every single one of us is unique, and those differences are meant to be celebrated and encouraged, instead of frowned upon. This love for me taught me to question things I didn't understand, instead of judging, because I learned those judgments had nothing to do with the person, but had everything to do with ME! In the asking, I have learned much about others.

As my self-discovery took place, I began to notice changes in me:

- I was becoming more confident... something I had a total lack of in the past.

- I was beginning to love and appreciate myself more.

- I was seeing how brilliant I really am... I always believed I wasn't very smart.

- I discovered a strength and determination I had no idea I possessed.

- I could begin to see the possibility of living a life I thought was only for others, and not for me.

- I was achieving things I had no idea I could... like becoming an author. I Co-authored my first book in 2017.

- My beliefs were changing. My belief in myself was increasing slowly but surely.

- I was breaking through multi-generational cycles that had been passed down... cycles I never thought to question. I saw how I had come to accept these cycles, as well as continue them without understanding how my life was being governed by these cycles that were no longer valid. And so much more!

SOME TOOLS YOU CAN USE:

1. Begin being curious about who you really are beneath the surface.

2. Don't be afraid to take time to discover the "real you"... who you are, what you like, etc.

5 JUDGING

My life up until this point had been based on judging others, as well as acknowledging the judgments others placed upon me. I thought this was a normal practice, until I learned that whatever I judged in someone else was in me too! This, I tell you, was a very difficult pill to swallow, and took a little bit of time to accept. What stands out in my memory is that I often referred to my ex-boss as an asshole. Every time I said this, my second mentor told me to take a look in the mirror. I would shrug it off and preferred to focus on the changes that were taking place within me instead. But in the background, a little part of me would process this information, even though I didn't want to accept it as true.

I don't know when the awakening in me began to take place, but I know that one day I was taking a walk and thinking about something my ex-boss had done that irritated me, when it struck me that I was in actual fact the asshole, due to my poor performance at work, and my negative attitude towards my job in general. I remember stopping in my tracks and verbally shouting, "No! I cannot be the asshole here... he is!" Needless to say, the evidence was now crystal clear that it was me! This, I tell you was the first of a few (putting it mildly) difficult pills I would be swallowing as my transformation journey progressed. I did however take a few weeks to process this and argue with myself. Eventually, I took *responsibility* for my actions and released the blame on my ex-boss.

The great thing about this powerful lesson (that whatever I'm judging is most likely something that is in me) is that I was able to change myself. And... yes, I still catch myself judging others every now and then, but I no longer hold onto those judgments, because I know now that they're a reflection of me. I now do my best to understand others, which has taught me so much about allowing people to be who they need to be, because our life journeys are unique to each of us individually. I AM who I AM, and they are who they are. I am doing my best to work on me, in order to become a better version of who I was previously.

I've seen firsthand how difficult it has sometimes been to fix the judgments in myself, and I know that I can't fix anyone else. I can only fix me! Seeing how difficult it has sometimes been to fix the judgments in me has shown me how to be more open and compassionate towards others, especially my children.

SOME TOOLS YOU CAN USE:

1. Begin to take note each time you judge others.

2. Ask yourself, if any of those judgments could possibly be in you?

3. Instead of judging others, try to look for something positive in them (their hair, eyes, smile etc... something easy to begin with.

6 INTERNAL HEALING

My healing journey was pretty tumultuous. Mostly because I didn't completely understand what was happening in the beginning, so I resisted a lot. I was also used to beating myself up a lot for not overcoming the things that needed to be healed within me, and for resisting the process. Another thing I didn't understand was that some of the things I needed to address had a few layers to them, like the anger in me. Sometimes, something I had worked on and believed to have healed would show up again. This frustrated me greatly, as I didn't know this is normal. Once I learned this can happen, I began to be kinder and gentler with myself.

Healing my internal wounds has been a refining process. I have often referred to the process as a diamond in the rough. The belief that I would emerge from the process as a beautiful, sparkling diamond of love and light kept me going through the tough times.

It was not easy to visit the pain of the past. After all, I had buried it so it could no longer hurt me, or so I thought. Some of the pain I had buried so deep within me that I had forgotten about it. One by one, the memories began to surface, and would not go away until I addressed them. My way of addressing these memories was to relive these painful moments. I allowed myself to feel the feelings of fear, sadness, shame, anger, turmoil, and whatever else came up. Then came the crying. Gut wrenching tears that would last for days on end. I called these tears "soul cleansing tears," because after I was all cried out, I would feel so much lighter and freer on the inside.

What I have learned from revisiting each one of the painful memories is that the past is long gone, and can no longer hurt me, unless I choose to hold onto the hurt and pain. I learned that the only thing that can continue to hurt me is my need to hold onto the memories and beat myself up for the way I use to be back then.

As I grew from facing the past, I learned to forgive myself for who I was. I learned to release the hold of the memories with great love and gratitude. I say love, because love is who I AM, and who I was ultimately returning to. Gratitude, because gratitude is a game changer. Also, because I was no longer the person I was back when each situation took place. I AM always grateful for the past, because I know now that I was doing the best I could for who I was at that time in my life, and what I knew back then. My past to me, is and always will be a part of the process of my transformation. I am grateful for it, because I now get to choose to be a better version of the person I was in the past!

I know how scary it is to face the pain of the past. I also know that every situation is different, and each person needs to address their situation in their own time. I encourage you with great love in my heart to let go of the past in your own time. Know that it IS possible to be free of ALL the pain bottled up inside of you. I AM living proof of this. Keeping the feelings bottled up, allows them to fester and blocks you from the greater blessings waiting for you... Blessings beyond your greatest comprehension!

Life has so much more to offer you on the other side of this pain. Internal freedom being one. When you are free internally, you then open yourself up to receive the amazing blessings God/Universe has to offer you. Being free internally, allows you to view yourself and the world through eyes of love.

Seeing yourself and the world through eyes of love is a profound experience, one I don't have the words for. It's an experience my heart desires for you to feel.

Please Note:

This Healing is a process and will be different for each person. What I do know from my own experience is resisting the process only makes it harder. Your initial response will be resistance, and that is completely ok. Take all the time you need to build up the strength to face it. Also know that you absolutely DO NOT have to go through this alone. I AM here to support you, as best as I can through this journey, should you need me.

Another incredible lesson I learned from healing the pain of the past was, keeping the pain buried wasn't helping me. Keeping it locked up inside was contributing to my beliefs about life, and dictating decisions I made. I AM not saying you have to tell the world about your pain, if you don't wish to share it, that is entirely up to you. What I am saying is, it is possible to free yourself from the bondage of living a life of pain.

SOME TOOLS YOU CAN USE:

1. Face the memories that come up. They are seeking to be released. You are braver than you think!

2. Know that each Healing process is different. Some things will be easier to face, heal, forgive, and release. Others, you will resist because the pain runs too deep, or because you are not yet ready to go through the process and let it go.

3. Be as gentle with yourself as you can be as you move through the process. There may be blood, sweat and tears... there were for me. The great news is, you will eventually get to the other side! Once you get to the other side, you will be happy you stayed the course.

4. Cry, scream, shout, run, dance, punch a pillow, etc. Do what you feel is right for you to release the pain (I cried a whole lot). Please try your best not to take it out on others. This may not be easy initially, but you will get there, as I did.

7 FORGIVENESS

"Forgiveness is the fragrance that the violet sheds on the heel that has crushed it." ~ **Mark Twain**

I have learned that forgiveness of self is equally as important as forgiveness of others. By forgiving yourself too, you open yourself up to the greater good that is available for you.

Learning to forgive myself was a profound lesson, as I had never heard of this before. I only knew about forgiving others, and even that needed some work, because I would forgive, but still hold onto the hurt. When you choose to forgive yourself, or others, it is best to release the hurt as well. Holding onto the pain and memory really doesn't serve you, and keeps you blocked off from the blessings waiting for you.

What I have learned for myself regarding the memories, is to look at how the situation shaped my life, and brought me to where I AM right now. This has certainly helped release any bitterness I kept in my heart.

I also began to understand that I cannot change the past, but I can change who I choose to be going forward. I learned how to forgive myself for who I was and what I had done in the past, as I began to understand that what I did in the past was a reflection of who I was at that time. The person I AM today has changed drastically. I know more about who I AM, and who I AM continuously striving to become. The person I was in the past, did the very best with the tools and knowledge I had at the time. The person I AM today is open to learning more about me, so I can show up as an improved version of me each day.

There are times I fall off track, but instead of beating myself up for it the way I did before, I look for the lesson in the current situation, and get right back on track. I have learned that getting back up, no matter how many times you get knocked down, is where your strength increases, and your belief in yourself builds!

I know without a doubt in my heart that my past does not define who I AM. It was part of my journey to transformation, and that version of me no longer exists!

I have done my best to ask for forgiveness from those I have hurt in the past. Some people are not ready to forgive me. I understand this and keep my heart open to receive their forgiveness once they feel ready. If they are never ready or, if the forgiveness is not forthcoming, I know that there is nothing I can do about that, as it's part of their journey.

What I can do is continue to work on me and keep doing the best that I can to improve who I AM, based upon my life lessons.

I have forgiven those who have hurt me. Some have not asked for my forgiveness, but I needed to forgive them, and release myself from the burden of the pain that I held onto for so long. It is liberating to be free of the bondage that pain held me in for so long. I know now that holding onto the pain of the past hurts me more and affects how I live my life going forward. It affects my relationships, and it affects the decisions and choices I make.

I share with you this piece I wrote on Forgiveness...

Forgive Yourself,
by Cheron Van Beek

Forgive yourself because you didn't know.

Forgive yourself because you don't know.

Forgive yourself because you are doing the best you can for
who you are right now.

Forgive yourself because you are trying to improve.

Forgive yourself for knowing what you are supposed to do,
But don't.

Forgive yourself because you are human and some days you
just need to be angry, sad, a total mess.

Forgive yourself for the moments you are human, knowing
that tomorrow you will try again.

SOME TOOLS YOU CAN USE:

1. Begin forgiving others. I recommend starting with the easy ones. Trust me, forgiveness sets you free of the stronghold the situation has on you.

2. Forgive yourself, for holding on to the stuff you hold onto. This too is freeing for you. Understand that at each given moment, you were doing the very best you could for who you were in that moment.

3. Ask for forgiveness of those that you have wronged (please understand that there is a possibility they may not be ready to forgive you... move on knowing that you did your part).

8 MONEY

In September 2018, the Universe limited my source of income. First, I was released from the job I had worked at for so long. Then I collected unemployment. During the period I collected unemployment, the process of healing and transformation had begun. The person I was at this particular time, still had lots to learn. Then the Employment Insurance Benefits came to an end.

Fear took hold of me, as I worried about how we were going to survive. We had signed a lease on a house, and the rent was double what we had been paying. How were we going to pay the rent and other bills that come with the house?

Then, I fell behind on my loan and credit card payments. The worry and fear put me in anger mode. This anger, I took out on my children which is something I am not proud of at all, but I now know that it was a part of my learning process. Most of the time when the bank called, I avoided the calls! I was so ashamed of being in this situation, as it was a first for me. Eventually, I realized that I could not hide from the bank forever, and sooner or later I'd have to face them. I then began answering the calls, and was open and honest with them. They in turn, were compassionate and put together a payment plan that helped me catch up with my arrears!

Needless to say, each month the Universe provided the money for the rent, food and household bills. I, on the other hand worked on my anger, because I really did not enjoy screaming, shouting and swearing at my children.

In this time, I learned that when I was in alignment and loving myself, the outbursts were less. The anger would pop up randomly, which I later learned was because it was rooted against my mom (chapter nine talks more on this).

Feelings of desperation added to my fear. I was desperate to generate an income, and tried to host a workshop, but this did not materialize. This brought on feelings of disappointment, being a failure, and sadness. I wanted to give up! Thankfully, I did not give up, but instead learned that I had to heal my relationship with money, as well as reassess my beliefs about money.

I tried money affirmations, to call money into my life, but this didn't work. Then one day I awakened to the fact that I felt inferior to people with more money than I had, and felt superior to those with whom I thought had less money than I did. Another awakening was that I believed money was the root of all evil, to which I later learned is not the case. It is people who use money for evil gain. I wished for money, but was afraid of what would happen if I actually had the wealth I desired like having to share it with others, gaining best friends who were only interested in my money. All this, I now know was a huge part of blocking the money from flowing to me. I also learned that I needed to release the desperation, shame and fear around my financial situation.

As I addressed my beliefs around money, I awakened to how money has ALWAYS shown up for me to pay the bills, etc. but I wasn't grateful for the money that showed up. I continuously spoke about how broke I was, and how I couldn't afford anything!

The day I had this awesome awakening, I thanked money for always being there for me, throughout my life. I thanked money for its faithfulness towards me, and I asked money to forgive me for treating it badly. I released my feelings of inferiority and superiority towards others and began repairing my relationship with money. In the process, I was able to release the old beliefs I'd had around money too!

Even though I began this work, I still held onto my fear of not having enough money. Through continuous work, and study on my part, I learned a new way of saying a money affirmation that worked for me. I was studying the book, **The Power of Your Subconscious Mind,** by Joseph Murphy (I highly recommend this book). In the book Joseph Murphy talks about different ways to attract money. The one that resonated with me was saying the word "wealth" to myself. I tried this, and found that it put me in a vibration of peace, which gave me the ability to see myself with the wealth I desired. I also began to understand that money is energy and needs to be circulated. I was now able to begin making plans of how I would share my wealth with others, without any fear of losing my wealth.

I was still not generating an income from my business, so a friend suggested I apply for Ontario Works (government assistance). I did, and was able to receive assistance right away, which helped alleviate a lot of the stress I'd had.

On the morning of my daughter's seventh birthday party, as I cleaned the house, I awakened to the wonderful realization that money was now flowing easily and effortlessly into my life. I now understood why the money was taken away from me...

I needed to heal my relationship with money, change my beliefs regarding money, to be humbled in order to be an effective Servant.

The greatest lesson I have learned from this was that I needed to release my *desperation* around the need for money. I learned not to judge others' financial situations (something I did a whole lot of). And I now had a genuine heart's desire to be able to share my great wealth with others, because I had experienced firsthand what it is like to have my privilege of money greatly limited.

Another beautiful lesson in self-love learned. I AM so deeply grateful for my life and all the lessons I have learned. Some of those lessons took time to get through, because I held onto them, as well as resisted what needed to be learned and healed. I know that I am a constant work-in-progress. The difference now, is that I strive to be a better person than I was the day before. Sometimes I fall of the track with this. I now know that this is the "human" in me! The great beauty is that I have learned not to beat myself up about falling off the track, as it's part of the process of growth and transformation. Getting back up is what truly matters! Each time I was knocked down, I would lay there, cry, scream and shout at my children, then I'd get back up! After countless times of rising again, I began to realize that every time I got back up, I got back up feeling stronger than I was before.

More Growth Towards Money

As I work on the book, I am tasked with asking my ex-husband if he could send us some extra money to get some stuff for the young ladies. I wasn't afraid to name the price of how much I would like. The old version of me, would have been very afraid of asking for the money, let alone naming the price I required, and I would have accepted an excuse (if one was given) too.

I awakened to how different I had now become. Before, when I needed to ask for money from anyone, I would feel fear, shame and guilt for asking. This would lead to me going into a very long explanation of why I needed the money. I was so insecure around asking for money, not to mention the limiting beliefs I had regarding money. I also did not feel deserving of receiving money, but always desired more than what I had at any given time.

I still desired more money, but found that now I wasn't as desperate as I was in the past. If I found money lying around, I picked it up, thanked money and rejoiced at the blessing of having found the money.

The day I sent the message to my ex-husband, I felt confident and deserving of receiving the extra money I had asked for... a totally new and different attitude. It feels so good to feel deserving of receiving money, and not being afraid of asking and naming the price! I feel I deserve and expect to receive it, without any fear or doubt.

I AM deeply grateful to my ex-husband for his generous heart, because it has certainly played a huge part in me arriving at this great awakening.

I remember growing up, we were poor and a number of times before school began, my younger sister and I would have to walk to my aunt's (my father's older sister) job to ask for money for school fees and to purchase school uniforms. So much shame filled my being each time we had to do this. My Aunt, God bless her, never complained or made us feel as if we owe her. She ALWAYS, ALWAYS came through for us, even though she had a family of her very own to take care of.

Today, I AM Grateful to be free of the fear and shame of asking for money! I see how I have changed once again, and grown even more! I know now, that I am ready to serve my Soul clients, without fear of charging what I believe I deserve for my services.

There are so many intricate details that have come up for healing on this transformation journey. I had no idea I had fear and shame around asking for money, because it is another shame I had buried so very deep within my core.

I AM grateful this came up before the book was done, so I could add this chapter in. I am grateful for the opportunity to heal and release something else from deep within me. I feel new, refreshed, ready and open to receive financial abundance that has been patiently waiting to come into my life.

SOME TOOLS YOU CAN USE (QUESTIONS YOU CAN ASK YOURSELF):

1. What are my beliefs about money?

2. What do I think of money?

3. How do I treat money?

4. Do I need to repair my relationship with money?

9 ANGER IN ME

I believe the anger in me towards my mom began when I was fifteen years old. This is how I remember my life being at a young age...

My mom was a single parent of four daughters, including me, and I am the oldest of all of us. As far as I can remember, life was good for all of us (even though we were poor, from my child perspective). Being the eldest, I often took care of my younger sisters.

I cannot speak for my mom, or my siblings, as I don't know their experiences, or how they perceive the situation. This is my story from my perspective of the events that took place, as well as my story of healing the pain, shame, guilt and feelings of abandonment within me. One thing I know is that the lives of my sisters and I changed when my mom began dating a man who had no children of his own.

At some point (not sure when exactly), my mom moved in with her boyfriend, but didn't take us with her. My memories round the next events are pretty vague. What I do remember is that my sisters and I were moved around a number of times. We lived with my grandfather (my mom's dad), one of my mom's cousins, and a friend of my mom. I do remember that my mom would visit us often, then go home to her boyfriend.

The memory that stands out to me in my mind, is the day my mom came to tell my sisters and I that my one sister and I would be moving to Bulawayo (the city our dad and his mom lived in at the time). I don't remember being given an explanation, or a choice in this matter. All I know is that for the first time in my life, my whole world as I knew it was falling apart, and there was nothing I could do about it (at least the person I was back then believed this). I was devastated by the turn of events... I didn't want to be separated from my two younger sisters, who had somehow become my children and responsibility in my mind. I don't think that my mom going to stay with her boyfriend affected me as much as having to leave my sisters behind. The pain that overcame me was too deep for my fifteen-year-old brain to comprehend. I had no idea what to do. I didn't want to move, as I was afraid for myself and my sisters. I was the protector of all of us (at least that's how I perceived it). My mom had left to be with her boyfriend, and I in turn believed I was now the mom of my younger sisters. A role and responsibility that was handed to me, then taken away just like that!

Burying this pain brought about feelings of deep anger towards my mom. An anger that would fester for well over thirty years of my life. I felt shame of having to move and leave my two younger sisters behind. I felt guilty at not being able to do anything about keeping us together. But most of all, I felt a deep sense of abandonment by my mom. There were also feelings of fear for this new life that lay ahead.

I was deeply terrified of change, of starting a new life (new school, new friends, etc.). The pain of this unexpected move cut deep, and I didn't know how to process it all. I did not know how to handle this excruciating pain, as well as the guilt, shame and feelings of abandonment (I felt abandoned by my mom, and I felt as if I had abandoned my two younger sisters I had to leave behind). I felt as if I had failed all of us! All these feelings were way too much for me to handle, so I buried them deep within the very core of my being. I then replaced those feelings with anger and resentment towards my mom and her boyfriend. I hid the anger and the pain, and focused on doing what I could to take care of my younger sister (the one I moved with) and myself. I don't remember my sister and I talking about our feelings, but I do know that the situation built a strong bond between us (a positive I wasn't aware of at the time).

When we moved to Bulawayo, my gran (father's mother) took care of my sister and me. She bestowed so much love upon my sister and I in the years we spent with her. A love I cherish deeply to this day! Fortunately for us, we had spent some school holidays with my gran and had one friend in Bulawayo. Another great blessing was, we went to the same school as our friend, who introduced us to her friends. Thus blossomed some great friendships that would take us on some pretty amazing adventures; some of which are best kept between us friends (wink, wink).

I stayed in Bulawayo for three years, then I moved back to Harare, where I stayed until I moved to Canada in October of 2011. My sister stayed an extra year to finish high school, then she too moved back to Harare. The move to Canada began to change me slowly but surely. I often joked that it is in Canada where I began to grow up. You see, when I lived in Harare, I was very reliant on my younger sister (the one I moved to Bulawayo with), her husband and his parents. I worked and lived on my own, with my oldest daughter, but depended heavily on my sister and her in-laws. When I came to Canada, I had to learn to depend on myself for the most part.

From the moment I found gratitude for the trial that came to change my life, I thought that was "my story." What I couldn't understand was why the story never seemed to completely resonate with anyone when I shared it.

I received compassion, love, support and so much more, but something was greatly lacking and I didn't know what. Fortunately, there was a lot of internal work, learning, growing, discovering and healing I needed to work on, so I didn't focus on the lack of connecting to others with my story.

The journey to reaching "my story" has not been easy to say the least. I know now, that ALL I endured and learned along the way was preparing me for the "greatest" healing to come. I AM deeply Grateful to the Universe for saving the very best for last!

I have to share with you that I did my very best to resist dealing with this profound healing. I resisted, because a greater part of me knew that in order to heal, I had to revisit the most painful part of my past, relive that pain, then release it with love and gratitude. This pain, I had buried in the deepest part of my core! There were so many layers to this pain that needed to be addressed, that I was really scared to face.

When I finally began to look into this pain, I would address one layer, process it, and cry for days on end. After I was all cried out, I would feel free of the pain, and believed I had healed this pain.

As I said, it wasn't after facing this pain a few times, that I began to understand how very deep the pain ran, and how many layers would need to be addressed, and re-addressed.

As I began to understand this, I began to have compassion towards myself. I didn't know how much this process would take out of me. I was mentally, and physically exhausted at times. But I was determined to get through each layer. Every time I healed one layer, I rose stronger within, more sure of myself, and more aligned with my soul.

Then came the moment I had to take responsibility for this pain. This, I resisted with all I had in me. I had spent my whole life placing blame on my mother, and I was not yet ready to release her from the blame and pain I felt within me! Thankfully the Universe is patient, and allowed me time and space to resist.

Writing my feelings out became a great source of comfort to me. Sharing my thoughts and feelings honestly with God/Universe helped too (something I learned is much better than resisting), like being honest about not knowing how to heal the pain, forgive my mom and myself, and take the responsibility for all of this!

Eventually the moment came when I had no choice but to begin the work on this anger in me. Even though I resisted working on this because I didn't want to relive that pain, I could no longer keep it buried. By this time, a part of me knew it was time to face the darkest shadow within me, and there was no way to avoid it.

My first step in addressing this anger was to tell myself it was a learned habit, which was true, but only partially. So, I decided I was going to "change" the habit. I worked extremely hard on changing this habit. I would be loving and kind to myself and my children for a while, but always the anger came back. Whenever the anger came back, my children would face the brunt of this anger. I really didn't like taking my anger out on my children, especially since I had grown and transformed so much. The transformation and the anger were not in alignment. Somehow I knew this, but kept up the "band aid" fix, because it seemed easier, instead of addressing the root (my anger towards my mom). I knew I had to address this anger towards my mom, but I was afraid of being judged if I spoke about it. I was also afraid to face my mom, and... myself! So I kept up the "band aid" approach for as long as I could.

Then one day I was speaking to my sister who is my Health and Wellness Coach about my anger. She offered me a session to delve into the problem. I agreed, and we set up an appointment for the following week. What I didn't know was this session would open up the wound, and once that wound was open, there was nothing left for me to do, but Heal it! The session was powerful! I cried ... a lot! In fact, I cried for a number of days straight. After a few days, I felt so good and free. I was deeply Grateful to be free of this anger once and for all, or so I thought...

As I mentioned earlier, this root ran deep! What I didn't know at the time was things I thought I'd healed and were free of, would pop back up. I was confused by this, which led to me being frustrated with myself, until I learned that this is the process of healing. Needless to say, my first response towards stuff that resurfaced was resistance! I was mad that this stuff had the audacity to show up again. I mean, how many times did I have to go through the same thing over and over again? On this journey of healing, if you don't heal something completely, it will continue to show up. Eventually, I learned this, and stopped resisting, and being angry with myself, and focused on healing from whatever resurfaced.

Before I did all of this, my next step was to set my determination on fixing my darling mom. I had no idea how I was going to accomplish this, but again, it seemed like an easier solution. I felt it would be easier than facing this pain inside of me... which was not going to be the case. Still, I had to at least give it a try, right? All the while, knowing full well, that I can ONLY fix and change ME!

I realize now, that I tried to fix my mom, because I was not only afraid to revisit the pain, but a part of me felt the need to hold onto these emotions.

So, I began writing in the hopes of releasing the pain. The words that formed on the sheet of paper told me I had to take responsibility for my feelings, because those feelings were mine alone, and that I needed to fix ME, NOT my mom! This was certainly not what I wanted to do! This pill was going to take some time to swallow!

Fortunately, I'd learned early on in this journey to swallow those difficult pills and take responsibility for my feelings. Still, I needed a couple of weeks to digest this one. After a couple of weeks processing this, I accepted my responsibility and once again began to work on healing this root cause.

Even though I had begun the work, bitterness, resentment and judgment towards my mom still filled my heart. I really didn't want to have these feelings anymore, but I continued to hold onto them like a prized possession.

As soon as I accepted my responsibility, I came across a teaching of the late Dr. Wayne W. Dyer. In this teaching, he had a lady share her story of overcoming her resentment and anger. This lady shared how she was honest with God/Universe that she would need help to overcome her feelings. After hearing her story, I began being honest with God/Universe about my feelings, and asked for help. No sooner did I do this, I began to feel lighter. It was a huge relief knowing I was being supported through this by God/Universe.

Now that I felt supported by God/Universe, I genuinely began to work on this healing. I found it rather difficult to release this pain, and it caused me some distress to say the least. Until I realized that I'd been holding onto this anger, pain and resentment for well over thirty years of my life, and it had now become a great source of comfort to me.

When I first realized this, I thought it was completely ridiculous. How could this possibly be a source of comfort? One of the powerful lessons I'd learned was to take time out to process stuff I was resisting... so process is what I did. The more I processed, the more I understood why I had resisted releasing all of this. After all, if I released these toxic feelings, what would I do with myself? Who would I be, if I released the anger within me? My soul, told me I'd be LOVE! I would then open myself up to loving myself and others more, as well as be able to spread that love!

I knew I had to release the anger, pain and resentment, in order to move forward with my life. As it stands at this time of writing, I am still processing all this. I continue working on healing this, and work on building a better relationship with my daughters. I want them to be able to tell me freely if I am not loving them the way they need me to. I also know that in this process of healing and releasing, I need to work on forgiveness.

I am a beautiful work-in-progress, and I now know that the "anger in me" is my story. I see now how all I have faced was preparing me for this, and greater things to come.

This healing has taught me how to love myself more. It has given me compassion for my mom. As I reflect on the turmoil of this process to healing the anger in me, I see my mom differently. I have reached a point of forgiving myself for ALL of this. I have forgiven my mom in my heart, because I understand that she did the very best that she could for me, based upon who she was. Knowing this, I know that I cannot continue to hold onto the feelings of pain, anger, resentment and judgment.

For a long time during this healing process, I struggled with how can I be a loving person, but not have a relationship with my mom? What I have since learned is that I needed to release my mom for this part of my journey in order to heal. I'm not sure when (if ever) the relationship will be reconciled. All I know is that for now this is the way it needed to be. A part of me desires to have a relationship with my mom again, and a part of me is not yet ready. I know not to force the situation, and for now, continue to focus on healing me!

I do know that people will have many different views on this, and the fear of being put down for releasing my mom held me back for the longest time. What I know now, is that this is "my life" and I have to do what I feel is right for ME. Having learned to take responsibility for my actions and choices has given me the courage to stand firm in my decision, regardless of the good opinion of others.

I AM deeply grateful for this anger towards my mom, because it led to me wanting something different for my life. It has helped me strive to be a better version of me, as well as change my parenting approach completely. I parent my two younger daughters in a completely different way to the way I parented my older daughter.

I see now that the anger in me was a guiding force to the love that is and always has been inside of me. Without this anger, I would not have the love for myself and my children that I have now. This love is different to the way I loved my children before. Before, I loved them on condition that they fit into the way I wanted them to be and behave. Now, I love each one of them for who they truly are. By loving them this way, I AM learning so much from them, as well as seeing so many remarkable qualities of them I wasn't aware of before.

As for my mom, I know I love her. I don't feel ready to reconcile my relationship with her just yet, as I am still releasing a lot of the negative perceptions I have had for so many years. I know that I have to take the time to Heal these perceptions, so that when I do feel ready, I can go in love and be open to the option of not being received, because I do not know my mom's journey.

SOME TOOLS YOU CAN USE:

1. Ask yourself, "why is this situation triggering anger in me?

2. What is this situation trying to teach me?

3. What do I need to heal and release?

4. Am I ready to face myself and this pain? Be honest with yourself... know that if you are not ready, that is fine. When the time is right for you, it will happen.

5. Breathe. Take a deep breathe through your nose. Hold it for a second. Release the breath through your mouth! Do this as often as needed. This is a practice I use throughout the day that helps me keep calm and balanced.

6. Take a "time out." This is another practice I have begun using (bear in mind that my children are old enough to understand this and be on their own for a few minutes while I calm down). I tell my children I need a "time out" and go outside or sit in my room. I find having my "time out," breathing, and asking myself the above questions really helpful.

7. If you do react in anger, please don't beat yourself up about it. Life happens! Understand that you are aware of this and have begun working on a new way of being, so there will be moments of anger! Focus on asking for Forgiveness, and whatever practice you found to be right for you.

8. YOU ARE BRAVER THAN YOU THINK! YOU CAN DO THIS!

10 PEACE

"If there is no enemy within, the enemy outside can do us no harm." ~ African Proverb

I've often heard people desiring world peace. I'd like to share that peace begins with YOU. In order for there to be world peace, each one of us needs to make "peace" within our very own selves. Only then can there be "world peace."

I know this, because for the better part of my life I was angry deep within me. The person I was back then only knew how to be angry. That anger would show up a lot ... especially towards my children. The person I was back then also didn't know that I needed to find peace within me, in order to make a change in the world.

My life transforming trial came to teach me that there is way more to life than the way I perceived life in general. It taught me that it was okay to change and break free from generational patterns. It opened my heart and mind to ME: A ME, I never knew existed. As I went through each refining process, I began to discover how exquisitely beautiful I AM.

That there was more to me buried deep within. The treasures I uncovered inside of me, were the REAL ME!

Slowly but surely I connected to my soul. Slowly but surely I faced the traumas and pain of the past. As I faced them, I was able to release them with great love and gratitude.

As I faced and released these traumas and pain (some took longer than others), I began to notice a freedom within me that brought "peace" to my heart, soul and body. A peace I'd never experienced before.

Know that this peace I speak about is available to YOU too! This peace I speak of can only come once you face whatever is inside of you (anger, pain, guilt, shame, hostility, etc.).

SOME TOOLS YOU CAN USE:

1. Ask yourself, how you can begin to make peace with
    You! The first answer that comes to mind, is exactly
    what you need to do!

11 MY BEAUTIFUL BODY

For most of my life, I have not appreciated my body. I always felt I was "fat" and wished to be thinner. I was also embarrassed by the cellulite on my thighs, and felt my hips were too big. I was also teased a lot about my hips when I was younger, which added to my dissatisfaction and gave me a complex. I body shamed myself at every opportunity I got. I was always unsatisfied with my body. Because I body shamed myself on a continuous basis, I taught my oldest daughter to shame her body too.

Then, I began my journey to self-love. When you love yourself, that includes ALL of you (body included). I worked on this, but always fell back into the habit of judging my body, and feeling self-conscious about my hips. I wasn't able to receive compliments about my hips when given.

Towards the beginning of 2019, I unexpectedly awakened to the fact that I had become an emotional eater. Emotional eating had become my coping method during my trial. It was in this moment my eyes and my heart were opened to the fact that I turned to junk food when faced with a problem. I then understood what an incredible job my body had been doing to support me through the dark years. I began thanking my body for the extra inches, and for keeping me healthy. I thanked every part of my body for working extra hard to keep me going when I was stressed and filling my body with junk food. I was still fixated on releasing the extra ten pounds. I even told my body I loved it, but this was not a whole truth. I did love my body, but still thought, "if I could release these ten pounds, I will be able to love my body more.

Then, I began working on being mindful of my eating, and working out. As soon as I started releasing the inches, I would reward myself with junk food. This resulted in weight gain, and me not liking my body all over again. This was a recurring cycle, for a number of years, until I finally awakened to this cycle.

Then I participated in a 5 Day Sugar Free Challenge. During the challenge, I was so good, but didn't release any weight, as I had so desperately hoped. This fixation with releasing the weight was too much, I know. I also know that what you focus on expands, so I began to ask my body what it was telling me by holding onto the weight. I asked myself what I was holding onto that needed to be released in order to get past this fixation.

I received my answer in the shower one day. My body was waiting for me to heal my relationship with it, to ask for forgiveness for all the guilt, shame and abuse I had put it through. My body wanted to be friends with me. My body wanted my love and appreciation, and for me to feed it with good food and good thoughts.

This day I slowly began to release my fixation on releasing the weight and being unsatisfied with my body. This particular day I asked my body to forgive me for everything I did in the past. I asked this with great love, appreciation and respect for my body. I forgave myself for my behaviour towards my body. I began moving forward giving love and appreciation to my body for its shape, size and all the hard work it does to keep me fully functioning (something I've taken for granted) and in perfect health each and every single day!

After this awakening, I made a decision to love my body at all costs. I worked on being more mindful of the treats I ate (I love treats and didn't want to deprive myself). I also drank more water and made a promise to myself to walk each day. On the days the weather did not permit me to walk outside, I would get up from writing and walk around the house. I set a daily goal on my fitbit for myself. Each morning when I woke up, I would give myself a great big hug and a kiss, then I would slide my hands from my head to my toes, thanking each part of my body (something I still do).

I also began running in the basement each morning, in addition to walking during the day. I would release some of the extra inches, then I'd reward myself by eating a whole lot of junk. Then, I'd stop working out, and beat myself up mentally, and eat more junk. This recurring cycle frustrated me greatly. I desperately wanted to love my body, but I couldn't, because I wasn't as "thin" as I wanted to be. I'd tell myself I love my body, then I'd catch a glimpse of myself in the mirror, and I'd be disappointed with myself for not eating better.

Even though I was in a recurring cycle, I would get back to working out and eating healthy after a while. Each time I got back into the running and eating healthy, I noticed a change in me. One day, I noticed I was tuning into the guidance of my body.

This was a huge turning point for me. I realized that my body was waiting for me to acknowledge how much it had done for me all my life. My body wanted a healthy relationship with me. This was pretty mind blowing! In this momentous moment, I began thanking my body for keeping me healthy throughout my life. I thanked my body for keeping me healthy during my crisis, and only giving me a few extra pounds to contend with, and not a sickness.

Even with this newfound appreciation, I was fixated on releasing ten pounds. The more I thanked my body, the more my body told me what it needed. I began working out again, but this time I realized how much I enjoyed working out. I saw this as an act of self-love and enjoyment, and less of a reason to release the weight. Then my body began guiding me on what to eat. Slowly but surely, I found that some of the junk food I once thought I'd never be able to live without wasn't as satisfying as it once was.

I began listening to the heeding of my body, and saw how much better I felt within myself when I did. I also began to love and honor my body just the way it is. I am able to wear a bathing suit without covering up, and walk around in that bathing suit with my head held high.

Reaching this point of deep love and appreciation for my body has been a rollercoaster ride. One I wouldn't change for anything.

I have managed to release my fixation and desperation with releasing the weight, which has brought me to a place of love for my body, and has given me internal peace.

I see that the extra inches gained were a significant part of my journey. A journey that has taught me so much, and brought about such a great transformation within me. A profound journey that has helped to shape and mold me into the great person I AM today. A person who continuously strives to be better and expand soulfully the way I AM supposed to.

It feels wonderful to be free of the pain, shame and limitations of the past. I love seeing life through eyes of love. Love is within each and every one of us. Love is also all around us. Self-Love has changed me so greatly and so powerfully.

This power I speak of is not a power that overcomes others to have them under your will. It is a power that gives me comfort, peace, assurance, joy and so much more. I have gained this power and strength by overcoming the darkness in my life!

<u>Thank You My Body</u>

Thank you body for loving me!

Thank you body for not giving up on me!

Thank you body for always taking great care of me behind the scenes.

Thank you for your love and loyalty towards me.

Thank you body for teaching me how to love, nurture, treat and take care of you.

Thank you my beautiful Body!

I release the lifelong complex I took on about my sexy hips. I release all the body shaming I did. I release my fixation to be ten pounds lighter. I love you my body, just the way you are!

SOME TOOLS YOU CAN USE:

1. Know that coming from a place of "desperation" is not going to get you the results you are looking for.

2. Always go easy on yourself and be kind to yourself in the things you verbalize and think about your body.

3. Let your body guide you on what is right for it..

12 I LOVE AND APPROVE OF MYSELF

Slowly, you will become aware of habits in your life that need to be changed. Slowly, you will begin to work on releasing the old habits, by practicing new habits. Then... one day, you will stop for a moment and see how the new habits have been installed, and notice the beautiful difference in you.

This is how I began to love and approve of myself. I used this Louise Hay Affirmation, and began working on me... slowly, but surely.

I have learned that it is imperative that I love myself first, for who I AM. If I found a habit that didn't align with me loving myself, I worked on releasing that habit and implementing a new one.

I learned that it is ok to take time for me. I needed "me" to recharge myself and fill my cup. I love reading, so I began reading again. This time, I began reading books that taught me more about how my mind works, how to Love myself more... books that I felt would help me become a better version of me.

I also learned to ask for help. In asking my children for help, I saw how I was teaching them responsibility. A number of times, I needed to swallow my pride and ask for financial assistance from the government, and my family. Having to ask for financial assistance taught me that it is ok to ask for help.

I learned how to judge myself less by focusing on the good qualities within me. I learned that when I judge others, I'm judging myself. This took a while to learn, as it was a pretty difficult pill to swallow. It took me a while to process this one. When I accepted it as true, I began to see myself and others differently. The beauty of this is, I stopped beating myself up in my thoughts, and began to be more loving and kind to myself in my head.

When you love and approve of yourself, you begin to overcome the many obstacles your life has. The more obstacles/blocks I overcame, the more clearly I saw the great beauty of me. I did all the internal work, like facing the darkness of my past. Being able to heal my fears from the past and release them was so freeing and liberating. It gave me confidence. It showed me how very strong and courageous I was internally. I AM a continuous-work-in-progress, and I love it. I love working on me. I love seeing myself grow bolder, and believe in myself more and more each day. I love seeing the changes that have taken place in me. I have come a very long way since 2012. I have changed. I have grown. I have learned countless beautiful life lessons. And... I continue to learn and grow. I continue to work on me. I AM the change I wish to see in the world! I AM the love I wish to see in the world. I AM the Light the world needs!

Self-love sets you free from societal expectations. Because you love yourself so much, you seek the approval of others less, and trust yourself and your intuition more.

SOME TOOLS YOU CAN USE:

1. "I love and approve of myself," is a Louise Hay Affirmation I use all the time. This really helped me learn to "love and approve of myself."

2. Take time for you (rest, read, go for walks, go for a run, soak in a bubble bath... whatever works for "you" time). Know that it is NOT selfish to take time for yourself. It's beneficial!

13 PAST RELATIONSHIPS

"YOUR past relationships never failed you. YOU failed them."

This was a message I received in my sleep in the early hours of a Sunday morning. In my sleepy state, I remember getting out of bed to write this down. A few hours later and fully awake, I went to get my notebook to expand on what I had written down earlier.

Well... when I looked at the above message, I was rather taken aback to say the very least. So far in my journey of growth, I have learned to take responsibility for my actions. I have also dealt with the past and released it. To be completely honest, I thought I was free of the past and now ready to move forward with my new chapter.

Receiving the above message threw me for a loop, and led me to revisit the past, and see how the person I was back then had failed my relationships.

To every relationship I failed in the past, I humbly ask for your forgiveness. To every relationship I failed in the past, I AM Grateful to be awakened to my failure, because this Awakening has shown me how to be a better person going forward.

For a brief moment, I was tempted to ignore this message, because it meant I would have to address me. From my experience, I know that burying the message instead of addressing it:

(1) puts me in bondage to my failures.

(2) the longer I put off addressing it, the more it festers into something more, that is in turn transferred to my children and others around me.

I no longer wish to be in bondage to the lessons that have been designed for me, so on the Monday, I made a decision to address this message. I AM very happy I did, because I feel so much better knowing this message came to show me how to be a better mother, friend, sister, cousin, aunt, etc. This exercise has made me love myself more.

This has taught me that every situation life has to offer is about me: My perception of the situation; whether I choose to react in anger, or respond in love. And the greatest lesson in love the situation has to teach me is that I AM the one I need to work on, in order to make the change.

This message I received from the Universe in the early hours of Sunday morning has allowed me to delve deep within. My initial reaction was bury it. I know now that what I bury festers. Going forward with my life, I no longer want to bury anything that shows up in my life to be healed.

I took Sunday to ponder the message received. On Monday, I believed I addressed the message. Tuesday the message came up again, so I knew I had not fully dealt with it. I was ok with this, as I believed I had already begun the process of healing.

I see too, that I needed more time to work on this message. On Tuesday, I had the opportunity to think about my actions. I take full responsibility for failing those I love. I wholeheartedly forgive myself for not only failing those I love, but for failing myself too.

I AM able to see those I failed differently. I honor them for their response to me failing them. If you are reading this book, and I have failed you in some way, I ask you to forgive me when you feel the time is right in your heart to forgive me. I acknowledge my failure to you. I acknowledge that while I was failing you, I was failing myself too.

Going forward with my life, I will do the best I can not to fail myself, or you. I use the powerful lessons learned from this to improve who I AM.

I see that it is all about me changing me, and working on the lessons learned that pertain to my life. But it is also about how I use those lessons learned. My heart's desire is to use these lessons in love to inspire others to change what they feel they may need to be changed in their lives.

I AM grateful to have had the opportunity to address this, and release it with love and gratitude.

14 DOUBTS AND FEARS

Have you ever had this voice inside of you, telling you to do something, but you do your very best to shut that voice out and stifle it?

I have had my fair share of those experiences. When I ignore that voice inside of me, I have felt uncomfortable, and unhappy with myself.

What I didn't know back then was, that voice is my soul directing my path. Today, I know this, and do my best to go with the guidance my soul offers.

For over a year now, I have known that writing sets my soul on fire. When I write, I come alive in a way that I can't really explain. But I have stifled the need to write. A few months ago, I awakened to the fact that writing is my gift from the Universe. I gratefully accepted this gift, and set off to write this book.

Along the way, doubts and fears began to pop up. This would lead to days of not writing. Then, I'd start writing again, and feel myself come alive again. Then... you guessed it, doubts and fears would pop up. A recurring cycle.

Then, I was on my 6AM Book Club call, and I started re-writing the outline for this book. As I wrote, I began to feel alive once again. When I don't write, I don't feel dead, I feel stagnant, or something. I do know that this has been part of the process of my growth. As I wrote, I found myself expressing those doubts and fears, and questioning them.

What I know now is that fear of being in the spotlight has been holding me back. I've had this fear before, but buried it. This fear has come back to revisit. This time, I know that I can no longer Allow this fear to hold me back. I have come too far to give up now.

I see clearly too, that doubts and fears have knocked me down a fair share of times. But each time I was knocked down, I used the time to process what had happened. I learned from each and every knock. Each time I got back up! I began to notice that each time I got back up, I got up stronger, wiser and more determined to keep moving forward.

I learned to celebrate my wins along the way, and I gave much gratitude for each situation, because I know each situation was being used to move me forward, one situation at a time. I know that every time I grow, doubts and fears will assail me, as I will be stepping into a newer version of me, as well as embarking on a new branch of my journey that is unknown. The person I AM today will do my best to welcome those doubts and fears, because I see now that all they are doing for me is keeping me locked in a situation that no longer fits who I AM. I know that at the right moment for me, I will be able to push through those doubts and fears, into something greater and more beautiful.

I would like you to know that doubts and fears will assail you too, when it's time to step into the unknown. It is what you choose to do with those doubts and fears that will define your life's journey!

In the beginning, I was afraid of all the things I thought could go wrong. None of those fears ever came to fruition, by the way. So, now I have been facing the fear of what could go right! It may sound crazy, but it is absolutely true. How AM I going to get through this? I ask myself. My soul answers, 'the same way you have been getting through all you went through! Moment by moment, with faith, knowing you are always fully supported!

I sit with this answer for a moment and let it sink in. I see how I got this far, by taking life moment by moment. Resting when I needed to. Falling off the track, and spending time there, then... rising stronger and more assured of who I AM. So, I can most certainly take the time to enjoy it all working out for me!

Doubts and fears are completely normal in the grand scheme of things, especially when you are Awakening to the beauty of who you really are. As you grow, and find out things about you, you were not aware of before. It is a most profound experience. YOU uncover so many beautiful treasures within you, that you had no idea you possessed. In order to uncover those treasures for yourself, you have to remove those walls of protection you have installed around yourself, because all those walls are doing is keeping you from discovering the true magnificence of YOU!

SOME TOOLS YOU CAN USE:

1. Know that doubts and fears are completely normal. Overcoming them is totally possible too!

2. What doubts and fears can you face and overcome today? Start small (if you need to, as this builds your confidence, and belief in yourself!

3. Overcoming your doubts and fears, shows you how brave and awesome you really are.

15 I AM SUCCESSFUL

All my life I have believed that in order to be successful I needed to have a degree and be wealthy financially. I have since learned there are many other areas in one's life to be wealthy... health, self-love, relationships and so much more!

As I drove to drop off my Income Reporting Statement at the Ontario Works office, it occurred to me that I had been so busy focused on one way of viewing success, I had almost missed how very successful I have been, and continue to be.

For at least four years now, I have been working on ME. Learning who I truly AM, improving my relationship with myself and my children, and so much more.

In all this time, I have managed to overcome the greatest trial of my life, and have seen changes in me I had no idea were even possible! That in itself is a major success! I have broken the cycle of generational habits, and I AM inspiring others to make the changes their lives need... another major success in my life!

The more I looked back at how far I have come, the more successes I have found to be humbly proud of. I began to see how every day activities I took for granted can be counted as successes in my life, because each day I work on being a better version of the person I was the day before.

Sometimes, I fall back into some of the old behaviours, but I have learned to be easy on myself. After all, I've had those behaviours for forty plus years. What I focus on is getting back into the new behaviours, because I know that the more I work on the new behaviours, the more they will become my way of life.

SOME TOOLS YOU CAN USE:

1. Make a list of your everyday successes. This will help motivate you to keep pushing through the moments you want to give up.

2. Each day, make a short list (1-6) items of stuff you'd like to do. Check each item off as you take care of them.

3. Believe in yourself! You are AWESOME!

16 SEEK THE LIGHT WITHIN YOU

For a number of months, I have been fascinated with the plants in our home. Mostly, I have been watching the Orchid and African Violets as they blossom. This year, they are both coming alive like never before. Last year, they did not appear to have as much growth, and they had way less buds than this year.

Then, I began to notice the succulents in the bathroom, but not quite seeing them. One cloudy day, I noticed how the succulents have been growing towards the light (they are on the window sill). When we first got them, they were upright. Now, they have grown to the side... leaning towards the light.

As I noticed this, I see how I have been growing towards the light of love within me. Each layer of pain, shame, anger, guilt, etc. I shed has opened my heart to the light of love within me, which in turn has opened my eyes to see love all around me.

I have done extensive internal work. Now I see that it is time to emerge from the shadows I've been hiding in and shine my light, so others may seek and find the light within themselves. I feel myself rising. My Soul is shining through my human existence. I feel different now... certainly different from the way I felt last year. I am rising! I am shining from the inside out! Radiating love and peace!

ABOUT THE AUTHOR

Cheron Van Beek is an inspirational force, successful teacher of self-love, professional speaker, and international bestselling author, who is passionate about helping others overcome their past struggles and step into the life they were meant to have.

Cheron is on a mission is to help others achieve greatness in their lives, make healthy choices and thrive even through difficult and challenging times.

Cheron is a highly sought after speaker and is available for:
- Speaking Engagements
- Workshops
- Webinars

Cheron can be reached at:
Email: cheron@cheronvanbeek.com
Instagram: @cheronvanbeek
Facebook: https://www.facebook.com/cheronvanbeek/

ACKNOWLEDGMENTS

To Carrie, thank you for all the work you have put into helping with editing the book, getting it formatted and published. You have gone above and beyond to help me with such a great accomplishment in my life. I could not have asked for a better Soul to work with! Thank you for keeping my voice alive in this book. Thank you for seeing greatness in me that helped to increase my Belief in myself.

To Mi, thank you for the gift of this amazing book cover, that spoke directly to my Soul. Thank you for knowing exactly what I needed. Thank you for Blessing the life of myself and my children so richly!

To my Sister Sam, you have been my greatest cheerleader! Thank you for being on this journey with me, through the good, the bad and the ugly! I absolutely love how you have celebrated my every success, and been my shoulder to cry on. I AM Grateful for how deeply you have Blessed my life!

Cheers to you three incredible ladies! I wish each one of you the greatest success life has to offer you! I love you all dearly, Cheron xox

Printed in Great Britain
by Amazon

50370081R00047